PRACTICAL
GODS

Also by Carl Dennis

PRACTICAL GODS

CARL DENNIS

PENGUIN POETS

PENGUIN BOOKS

Published by the Penguin Group
Penguin Putnam Inc., 375 Hudson Street,
New York, New York 10014, U.S.A.
Penguin Books Ltd, 27 Wrights Lane,
London W8 5TZ, England
Penguin Books Australia Ltd, Ringwood,
Victoria, Australia
Penguin Books Canada Ltd, 10 Alcorn Avenue,
Toronto, Ontario, Canada M4V 3B2
Penguin Books (N. Z.) Ltd, 182–190 Wairau Road,
Auckland 10, New Zealand

Penguin Books Ltd, Registered Offices:
Harmondsworth, Middlesex, England

First published in Penguin Books 2001

5   7   9   10   8   6

Page ix constitutes an extension of this copyright page.

LIBRARY OF CONGRESS CATALOGING-IN-PUBLICATION DATA
Dennis, Carl.
Practical gods / Carl Dennis.
p. cm.
ISBN 0-14-100230-1 (pbk. : alk. paper)
I. Title.

PS3554.E535 P73 2001
811'.54—dc21   2001034637

Printed in the United States of America
Set in Sabon
Designed by M. Paul

For Lynne Cohen
and Anne Shapiro

ACKNOWLEDGMENTS

Thanks are due to the editors of the following magazines, in which some of the poems first appeared:

American Poetry Monthly ("More Art")

American Poetry Review ("Audience")

American Scholar ("Eurydice")

The Nation ("To a Pagan")

The New Republic ("Bashō," "Bishop Berkeley," "History," and "On the Bus to Utica")

Pivot (*"Gelati"*)

Poetry ("Eternal Life," "Eternal Poetry," "Glory," "Jesus Freaks," "Not the Idle," "Progressive Health," "Prophet," "Saint Francis and the Nun," "School Days," and "Sunrise")

Prairie Schooner ("The Serpent to Adam")

Salmagundi ("The God Who Loves You," "Infidels," "The Lace Maker," "A Letter from Mary in the Tyrol," "Progress," and "View of Delft")

Tri-Quarterly ("May Jen")

I also would like to thank the Rockefeller Center for sponsoring a stay at Bellagio and the Yaddo Corporation for sponsoring stays at Saratoga.

Finally, I would like to thank the generous friends who gave me valuable criticism on all these poems: Charles Altieri, Thomas Centolella, Alan Feldman, Mark Halliday, and Martin Pops.

CONTENTS

PRACTICAL
GODS

A PRIEST OF HERMES

The way up, from here to there, may be closed,
But the way down, from there to here, still open
Wide enough for a slender god like Hermes
To slip from the clouds if you give your evenings
To learning about the plants under his influence,
The winged and wingless creatures, the rocks and metals,
And practice his sacred flute or dulcimer.

No prayers. Just the effort to make his stay
So full of the comforts of home he won't forget it,
To build him a shrine he finds congenial,
Something as simple as roofed pillars
Without the darkness of an interior.

If you're lucky, he'll want to sit on the steps
Under the stars for as long as you live
And sniff the fragrance of wine and barley
As it blows from the altar on a salty sea breeze.
He'll want, when you die, to offer his services
As a guide on the shadowy path to the underworld.

Not till you reach the watery crossing
Will he leave your side, and even then
He'll shout instructions as you slip from your shoes
And wade alone into that dark river.

SAINT FRANCIS AND THE NUN

The message Saint Francis preached to the birds,
Though not recorded, isn't beyond surmising.
He wanted his fellow creatures to taste the joy
Of singing the hymns he sang on waking,
Hymns of thanksgiving that praised creation.
Granted, the birds had problems with comprehension,
But maybe they'd grasp enough of his earnest tone
To feel that spring shouldn't be taken lightly.
An audience hard to hold, to be sure,
With a narrow attention span, a constant fluttering,
But a lot less challenging than the nun he counseled
Only this morning, a woman still young,
Dying slowly in pain, who asked him
Why if her suffering had a purpose
That purpose couldn't be clarified in a vision.
Why not at least some evidence
That the greater the suffering reserved for her
The smaller the portion reserved for others?
What a balm to be able to think as Jesus did,
That with every difficult breath of hers
Patients in sickbeds around the world
Suddenly found they were breathing easier.
What a relief for Saint Francis these birds are,
Free of the craving for explanation, for certainty
Even in winter, when the grass is hidden. "Look!"
He calls to them, pointing. "Those black specks
There in the snow are seed husks. Think
As you circle down how blessed you are."
But what can he point to in the nun's spare cell
To keep her from wondering why it's so hard
For the king of heaven to comfort her?
All she can manage now is to hope for the will
Not to abandon her god, if he is her god,

In his hour of weakness. No time to reply
To the tender homily at her bedside
As she gathers all her strength for the end,
Hoping to cry out briefly as Jesus did
When his body told him he was on his own.

Department Store

"Thou shalt not covet," hardest of the Commandments,
Is listed last so the others won't be neglected.
An hour a day of practice is all that anyone
Can expect you to spare, and in ten years' time
You may find you've outgrown your earlier hankering
For your neighbor's house, though his is brick
And yours is clapboard, though his contains a family.
Ten years of effort and finally it's simple justice
To reward yourself with a token of self-approval.

Stand tall as you linger this evening
In the sweater section of Kaufmann's Department Store
By the case for men not afraid of extravagance.
All will go well if you hold your focus steady
On what's before you and cast no covetous eye
On the middle-aged man across the aisle
In women's accessories as he converses quietly
With his teenaged son. The odds are slim
They're going to reach agreement about a gift
Likely to please the woman they live with,
Not with the clash in what they're wearing,
The father dapper in sport coat and tie, the son
Long-haired, with a ring in his ear and a shirt
That might have been worn by a Vandal chieftain
When he torched a town at the edge of the Empire.

This moment you covet is only a truce
In a lifelong saga of border warfare
While each allows the other with a shake of the head
To veto a possibility as they slowly progress
From umbrellas to purses, from purses to gloves
In search of something bright for the darker moments

When the woman realizes her life with them
Is the only life she'll be allotted.

It's only you who assumes the relief on their faces
When they hold a scarf to the light and nod
Will last. The boy will have long forgotten this moment
Years from now when the woman he's courting
Asks him to name a happy time with his dad,
A time of peaceable parley amidst the turmoil.
So why should you remember? Think how angry
You'll be at yourself tomorrow if you let their purchase
Make you unhappy with yours, ashamed
Of a sweater on sale that fits you well,
Gray-blue, your favorite color.

NOT THE IDLE

It's not the idle who move us but the few
Often confused with the idle, those who define
Their project in life in terms so ample
Nothing they ever do is a digression.
Each episode contributes its own rare gift
As a chapter in *Moby-Dick* on squid or hardtack
Is just as important to Ishmael as a fight with a whale.
The few who refuse to live for the plot's sake,
Major or minor, but for texture and tone and hue.
For them weeding a garden all afternoon
Can't be construed as a detour from the road of life.
The road narrows to a garden path that turns
And circles to show that traveling goes only so far
As a metaphor. The day rests on the grass.
And at night the books of these few,
Lined up on their desks, don't look like drinks
Lined up on a bar to help them evade their troubles.
They look like an escort of mountain guides
Come to conduct the climber to a lofty outlook
Rising serene above the fog. For them the view
Is no digression though it won't last long
And they won't remember even the vivid details.
The supper with friends back in the village
In a dining room brightened with flowers and paintings
No digression for them, though the talk leads
To no breakthrough. The topic they happen to hit on
Isn't a ferry to carry them over the interval
Between soup and salad. It's a raft drifting downstream
Where the banks widen to embrace a lake
And birds rise from the reeds in many colors.
Everyone tries to name them and fails
For an hour no one considers idle.

GELATI

These songs from the corner church,
Wafting through the window this August morning,
Lift the job of sanding my scarred oak bookcase
From a three, on a ten-point scale of joy,
To at least a four. Not a bad grade
For an enterprise mainly practical, preparing a site
Fittingly handsome for the noble shelf-load
Of Roman Stoics whose sensible pages,
Stacked now on my speakers, don't register on the joy chart.
A cold wind blows from their doctrine that a virtuous life
Is in harmony with the cosmos—the cold, companionless cosmos
That never comes through when you need a friend.
No wonder the early Christians won followers.
No wonder their living descendants sound joyful still
As they proclaim that even here, near the corner
Of Hodge and Elmwood, the soul may be quickened.

These singers have had a brush with vision
Denied me so far, though once, on the Appian Way,
Three miles outside of Rome, after I'd walked for hours,
Inspecting the roadside tombs, alone, in the heat of August,
Wishing I'd brought a water jug, ready to turn back,
A man pushing a cart suddenly staged an advent
As he intoned, *"Limonata, gelati,"* as if to a crowd
Though the road was empty. An old man
With a bright escutcheon of ice cream staining his apron,
Proclaiming that to ask is to have for the lucky few
Who know what to ask for.

For a minute it seemed the Bureau of Joy was calling
About a windfall blowing my way to guarantee
An eight or nine on the joy chart even if many wishes
Down on my list wouldn't be granted.

Today I seem to be focusing on my wish to sand
And stain and varnish my bookcase, a job that a monk
Who specializes in repetition might embrace as a ritual.
Let the moment expand, he says to himself,
Till time is revealed to be delusion.

For me, here in the passing hour,
The wind-borne singing brightens the moment
However faintly it enters, however it might be improved
By the brighter acoustics of the New Jerusalem.
And now it's time for a string quartet in a new recording.
And now it's time for the baseball game on the radio.

Whether the players regard the sport as joy
Or simply as work, the crowd seems alive
With the wish to compress a lifetime
Down to a single sitting. Now for the task
Of brushing the varnish on with a steady hand
While the crowd goes wild in the bottom of the ninth
As the man on first steps off the bag, a rookie
Who'll seem a savior if he gets home.

TO A PAGAN

It's sad to see you offer your prayers to the sun god
And then, when you really need him, discover too late
That though he's willing to help, other gods more potent
Decide against him. It's too late then to regret
You didn't invest your trust where we've invested.

Join us, and if help doesn't arrive at once,
At least the deputy angel assigned your district
May hear your groans in the wind and track them
Down to your attic apartment in the outskirts
And mark the coordinates on her map.

Then she's off on the long trek through the voids
To report the crisis. Imagine the vault of the stars
As a tundra stretching away for a million miles
Without so much as a hut for shelter,
Without a tree or a bush for a windbreak.

Imagine how lonely she is as she builds a fire
Of tundra grass in the mouth of a cave,
A fire that proves too small and smoky
To warm her icy plumage. Then add her voice
As she quakes a psalm to keep up her spirits.

Dwelling on her, your heart will fill with compassion
And you'll want to cry out, "Great friend, I'm thankful
For all you suffer for my sake, but I'm past help.
Help someone more likely to benefit," the prayer
Of a real convert, which is swiftly answered.

HISTORY

I too could give my heart to history.
I too could turn to it for illumination,
For a definition of who we are, what it means to live here
Breathing this atmosphere at the end of the century.
I too could agree we aren't pilgrims
Resting for the night at a roadside hermitage,
Uncertain about the local language and customs,
But more like the bushes and trees around us,
Sprung from this soil, nurtured by the annual rainfall
And the slant of the sun in our temperate latitudes.

If only history didn't side with survivors,
The puny ones who in times of famine
Can live on nothing, or the big and greedy.
If only it didn't conclude that the rebels who take the fort
Must carry the flag of the future in their knapsacks
While the rebels who fail have confused their babble
With the voice of the people, which announces by instinct
The one and only path to posterity.

The people are far away in the provinces
With their feet on the coffee table
Leafing through magazines on barbecuing and sailing.
They're dressing to go to an uncle's funeral,
To a daughter's rehearsal dinner. They're listening,
As they drive to work, to the radio.
Caesar's ad on law and order seems thoughtful.
Brutus's makes some useful points about tyranny.
But is either candidate likely to keep his promises?

When ice floes smashed the barges on the Delaware
And Washington drowned with all his men, it was clear
To the world the revolt he led against excise taxes

And import duties was an overreaction.
When the South routed the North at Gettysburg
It was clear the scheme of merchants to impose their values
On cotton planters was doomed from the start
Along with Lincoln's mystical notion of union,
Which sadly confused the time-bound world we live in
With a world where credos don't wear out.

School Days

On the heart's map of the country, a thousand miles
May be represented by a quarter inch, the distance
Between St. Louis and a boarding school in Massachusetts
Where the son will be taught by the same teachers
Who taught his father and will reappear Christmas
At Union Station singing his father's songs.

Likewise the distance walked by an immigrant mother
From the tenement on Locust to the school on Seventh
Equals the distance on the heart's map of the world
Between the Volga and the Mississippi.

Now she's left the children at the school door
And has watched them enter a country she'll never visit
From which they'll return this evening with stories
She won't be able to understand. And on weekends,
When she and her husband fill their one big room
With the clatter of piecework, the children wait for a seat
In the reading room of the Cass Avenue library
Where a book is a ship, its prow pointed toward Ithaca.

A thousand kisses to you, Miss Winslow, senior librarian,
With a slice of poppy-seed cake that mother made
For your help in boarding and raising the sails.
Now for the lotus-eaters and witches, princesses, gods,
Not one of which leaves Odysseus at a loss for words.
And all the words in English, a language stiff as a stone
On the tongue of the oldsters but flexible for the children.

What skill could be more useful than making a stranger
A friend with a single speech or tricking a giant
Eager to eat you? The boring parts can be skimmed

Like the trip to shadow land, where the hero has to sit still
And listen to the sad stories of shadows.

Three times he tries to embrace his mother,
Who pined away with longing for her lone son
Wandering far from home, buffeted by the sea god.
Three times he embraces only air.

GLORY

A moment of glory every once in a while
Isn't too much to expect, though it isn't likely
To reach me today. Only an hour till bedtime
As I sit in the living room watching a family movie.
Here is the comfort of familiar shadows
But not the glory of leading those shadows
Out of the flickering dark into the living present.
A distinction I need to keep clear
If I'm to claim the modest glory of honesty.

The sight of my cousins, uncles, and aunts
Huddled around the cake with my parents
On my seventh birthday shows how cherished I was,
A boy likely to grow to manhood
At ease with himself, confident of his gifts,
Daring the loneliness required by causes
Gloriously unlikely to triumph, which by now
I should be able to name more readily.

At least with birthdays like this to fall back on,
I can be strong enough to confront my failings,
Beginning with the pleasure I took in being coddled
More than my brothers were by those who mattered.
And if that memory leaves me feeling guilty,
It shows I'm not indifferent to justice.
And isn't regard for justice a notable virtue?

If that's not enough for a day's quota of glory,
I can show the film in reverse and watch an uncle
Bring an empty fork to his mouth and remove it
Mounded with cake; I can watch the forkfuls

Arrange themselves on the plates as slices
Pointed into the past to defy time's arrow.

And when the cake's restored, the birthday child
Blows the candles to flame with his hot breath.
And here's mother taking a match to unlight them.
And here's father smiling as he backs the cake to the kitchen
To box it and send it off to countries less fortunate
Whose inhabitants haven't learned to create from nothing.

PROPHET

You'll never be much of a prophet if, when the call comes
To preach to Nineveh, you flee on the ship for Tarshish
That Jonah fled on, afraid like him of the people's outrage
Were they to hear the edict that in thirty days
Their city in all its glory will be overthrown.

The sea storm that harried Jonah won't harry you.
No big fish will be waiting to swallow you whole
And keep you down in the dark till your mood
Shifts from fear to thankfulness and you want to serve.
No. You'll land safe at Tarshish and learn the language
And get a job in a countinghouse by the harbor
And marry and raise a family you can be proud of
In a neighborhood not too rowdy for comfort.

If you're going to be a prophet, you must listen the first time.
Setting off at sunrise, you can't be disheartened
If you arrive at Nineveh long past midnight,
On foot, your donkey having run off with your baggage.
You'll have to settle for a room in the cheapest hotel
And toss all night on the lice-ridden mattress

That Jonah is spared. In the space of three sentences
He jumps from his donkey, speaks out, and is heeded, while you,
Preaching next day in the rain on a noisy corner,
Are likely to be ignored, outshouted by old-clothes dealers
And fishwives, mocked by schoolboys for your accent.
And then it's a week in jail for disturbing the peace.
There you'll have time, as you sit in a dungeon

Darker than a whale's belly, to ask if the trip
Is a big mistake, the heavenly voice mere mood,

The mission a fancy. Jonah's biggest complaint
Is that God, when the people repent and ask forgiveness,
Is glad to forgive them and cancels the doomsday
Specified in the prophecy, leaving his prophet
To look like a fool. So God takes time to explain
How it's wrong to want a city like this one to burn,
How a prophet's supposed to redeem the future,
Not predict it. But you'll be left with the question
Why your city's been spared when nobody's different,

Nobody in the soup kitchen you open,
Though one or two of the hungriest
May be grateful enough for the soup to listen
When you talk about turning their lives around.
It will be hard to believe these are the saving remnant
Kin to the ten just men that would have sufficed
To save Gomorrah if Abraham could have found them.

You'll have to tell them frankly you can't explain
Why Nineveh is still standing though you hope to learn
At the feet of a prophet who for all you know
May be turning his donkey toward Nineveh even now.

DELPHI

Though I don't believe in oracles, I'm encouraged
By those who do, by their certainty that the future,
However narrow, isn't so closed as the past.
Options appear to persist for the passengers
Disembarking at the port of Corinth, persist as they rest
Before the jolting donkey ride up the mountain
And the long wait for their turn on the porch of the temple.

The farmer fresh from his farm on the island of Melos
Can't predict what the priestess will answer
When asked the wisest policy toward his son
Though he knows what he wants her to say:
That the boy has studied enough in Athens,
That another year means losing him to philosophy
When he ought to be home to help with the harvest.

The father listens with a mind as open
As he can make it when Apollo's servant,
Her eyes shut tight, her lips foam-flecked,
Mutters and moans in a voice not hers
Words that even to her are a mystery.

As for me, my only oracle is my notebook
Open on the kitchen table to a page divided
Straight down the middle with a heavy line.
If the arguments on the left-hand side
Outnumber those on the right, the left-hand path
At the fork ahead should be my preference
Unless the arguments on the right, however few,
Appear more beautiful, their truth more piercing.

And wouldn't that difference mean
That the right-hand path is the one I believe

An oracle would confirm if oracles existed?
The path that would lead me to the brighter good,
Me and the rest of the world worth helping,
My first choice, not my distant second.

INFIDELS

All that stands between us and the happiness
We know we deserve are the infidels,
Those pushing ahead in line at the market,
Making us wait while they haggle over pennies.
Once we ask them to leave we'll have time to spare
For mending porch screens at our own sweet tempo
Or lingering in our gardens.

Just the infidels and their oily, poppy-seed smiles
And promises that seduce our customers,
Even the canniest. Once they're out of the way
We'll have all the money we need for extras—
Trips to the sea and trips to the mountains.
Our children then won't whine to be elsewhere.
Our wives won't compare the lonely vistas
To the cozy photographs in brochures.

Then the land will be ours, all of it, forever,
This land of saints, heroes, and sages
Who now must conceal themselves indoors,
Away from the smoke spewed by the greasy stoves
Of the infidels. Then our prophets, strolling the streets,
Will explain how till that moment we lived in exile,
In Babylon, in a babel of foreign voices.

Then we'll be celebrants, not complainers,
Painters who gaze from their windows to find the crowd
Beautiful in the twilight, the flow of office workers
And factory hands all moving together
As they never could in times like these

When swarms of infidels push against traffic,
Hawking their trays of garish ties and sashes.

Let them go elsewhere, them and their hints
That our lives without them are doomed to be drab,
Lies they're far too cunning to utter openly.

PRIDE

A danger on many lists, but on mine
The best protection I have when I get an inkling
Of what it means to be shut forever
Inside one person, the windows barred.
Pride that proclaims to me and my kind
That the self isn't so small as it seems,
Just the small corner we're standing in,
Just this moment, which contains only a fraction
Of all we are. Look up, says pride, at the misty ceiling;
Look up ahead where the far wall rises
Covered with tapestries it will take a lifetime
To admire with the focused attention that they deserve.

Take pride away, and envy would scale our ramparts
Unopposed and force us to sign the papers
Declaring the rooms of houses other than ours
Far more inviting, more spacious and sunny,
The furniture chosen with taste that we can't muster,
The guests over there not only more interesting
But more generous than the tribe of gossips
And climbers crowding our anterooms.

O pride, O sweet assurance we're first,
May the dreams you provide us with always allow us
To ride in triumph through a grateful Persepolis
Certain we've earned the shouts of the crowd,
Certain the queen by our side isn't deluded
To love us best, just enlightened beyond her years.
Her gaze pierces to a trove of virtues
Hidden even from us, and will teach us
How wrong we've been to consider her heart
More cramped in its movements now that it beats for us,
Now that it's ours.

On the Bus to Utica

Up to a year ago I'd have driven myself to Utica
As I've always done when visiting Aunt Jeannine.
But since last summer, and the bad experience in my car
With aliens, I prefer bus travel. Do you believe
In creatures more advanced than we are
Visiting now and then from elsewhere in the universe?
Neither did I till experience taught me otherwise.
It happened one night last fall after the Rotary meeting.
I'd lingered, as chapter chairman, to sort my notes,
So I wasn't surprised when I finally got to the lot
To find my car the only one there, though the shadows
Hovering over it should have been a tip-off
And the strong odor I had trouble placing—
Salty, ashy, metallic. My thoughts were elsewhere,
Reliving the vote at the meeting to help a restaurant
Take its first steps in a risky neighborhood.
So the element of surprise was theirs, the four of them,
Three who pulled me in when I opened the door
And one who drove us out past the town edge
To a cleared field where a three-legged landing craft
Big as a moving van sat idling. In its blue-green light
I caught my first good look at their faces. Like ours,
But with eyes bigger and glossier, and foreheads bumpier
With bristles from the eyebrows up, the hair of hedgehogs.
No rudeness from them, no shouting or shoving.
Just quiet gestures signaling me to sit down
And keep calm as we rose in silence to the mother ship.
I remember the red lights of the docking platform,
A dark hall, a room with a gurney where it dawned on me
Just before I went under there would be no discussions,
No sharing of thoughts on the fate of the universe,
No messages to bring back to my fellow earthlings.
When I woke from the drug they'd dosed me with

I was back in the car, in the Rotary parking lot,
With a splitting headache and a feeling I'd been massaged
Hard for a week or two by giants. Now I feel fine
Though my outlook on life has altered. It rankles
To think that beings have reached us who are smugly certain
All they can learn from us is what we can learn
From dissecting sea worms or banding geese.
Let's hope their science is pure at least,
Not a probe for a colony in the Milky Way.
Do you think they've planted a bug inside me?
Is that why you're silent? Fear will do us more harm
Than they will. Be brave. Be open.
Tell me something you won't confide to your friends
Out of fear they may think you strange, eccentric.
If you're waiting for an audience that's more congenial,
More sensitive than the one that happens
To be sitting beside you now on this ramshackle bus,
I can sympathize. Once I waited too.
Now you can see I take what's offered.

Jesus Freaks

The approval they get from above is all they need,
So why should they care if they offend me
Here in the parking lot of the Super Duper, my arms full,
By stuffing a pamphlet or two in my pocket?

No point in shouting at them to keep back
When they're looking for disapproval. No reason
For them to obey the rules of one of the ignorant
Who supposes the perpetual dusk he lives in

Sunny noon. Their business is with my soul,
However buried, with my unvoiced wish for the truth
Too soft for me to catch over the street noise.
Should I rest my packages on my car a minute

And try to listen if I'm sure they really believe
They're vexing me in my own best interest?
To them I'm the loser they used to be
When they sweated daily to please themselves,

Deaf to their real wishes. Why make it easy for me
To load the trunk of my car with grocery bags
When they offer a joy that none of my purchases,
However free of impurities, can provide?

Their calls to attention shouldn't sound any more threatening
Than the peal of a church bell. And if I call
On the car phone to lodge a complaint,
Jail will seem to them the perfect place to bear witness

In this dark dominion where Herod rules.
In jail, but also guests at a banquet, while I,

They're certain, stubbornly stand outside
Shivering in the snow, too proud

To enter a hall not of my own devising
And warm myself at a fire I didn't light
And enjoy a meal strangers have taken pains with.
Yes, the table's crowded, but there's room for me.

THE SERPENT TO ADAM

Just as Prometheus, the compassionate god,
Stole to deliver man from darkness,
So for your welfare I named the forbidden tree
The tree of knowledge. And just as he understood
The punishment that was bound to follow,
The rules of Olympus being clearly posted,
So I was ready to drag my trunk through the dust
Toward the glow of your first campfire.
My loss would be far outmatched by the joy
I'd feel in the company of my new-made equals.
At last a chance for serious conversation
As we planned together a home in the wilderness
Fit for creatures who know good from evil.

No wonder I was stunned by your kicks and curses.
No wonder I was wounded in more than my body
As I scuttled back to the dark, dodging your stones.
Nothing could ever make you happy again
Now that the gardener didn't dote on you
And you'd have to fend for yourself,
Grow your own food and cook it,
Standing close to the fire to fend off cold.

That was your real crime, not disobedience:
To make me, a being hopeful by nature,
Into a slinking creature of holes and crevices,
My talents wasted, my soul so embittered
I was glad when I lost my lizard ears.
A relief not to hear anymore your wind-borne
Misty laments from the valley settlements.
A thousand sighs for an Eden that didn't suit you
And none for the Eden we might have made.

VIEW OF DELFT

In the view of Delft that Vermeer presents us
The brick facades of the unremarkable buildings
Lined up at the river's edge manage to lift the spirits
Though the sky is cloudy. A splash of sun
That yellows some gables in the middle distance
May be enough to explain it, or the loving detail
Vermeer has given the texture of brick and stone
As if he leveled each course with his own trowel.
Doubtless stones in Cleveland or Buffalo
May look like this on a day when the news arrives
That a friend is coming to visit, but the stones in the painting
Also put one in mind of the New Jerusalem,
A city we've never seen and don't believe in.
Why eternal Jerusalem when the people of Delft
Grow old and die as they do in other cities,
In high-ceilinged airy rooms and in low-beamed
Smoky basements, quickly, or after a stubborn illness,
Alone, or surrounded by friends who will soon feel Delft
To be a place of abandonment, not completion?
Maybe to someone returning on a cloudy day
After twenty years of banishment the everyday buildings
Can look this way or to someone about to leave
On a journey he isn't ready to take. But these moods
Won't last long while the mood in the painting
Seems undying, though the handful of citizens
Strolling the other side of the river are too preoccupied
To look across and admire their home.
Vermeer has to know that the deathless city
Isn't the Delft where he'll be walking to dinner
In an hour or two. As for your dinner, isn't it time
To close the art book you've been caught up in,
Fetch a bottle of wine from the basement, and stroll
Three blocks to the house where your friend is waiting?

Don't be surprised if the painting lingers awhile in memory
And the trees set back on a lawn you're passing
Seem to say that to master their language of gestures
Is to learn all you need to know to enter your life
And embrace it tightly, with a species of joy
You've yet to imagine. But this joy, disguised,
The painting declares, is yours already.
You've been longing again for what you have.

A CHANCE FOR THE SOUL

Am I leading the life that my soul,
Mortal or not, wants me to lead is a question
That seems at least as meaningful as the question
Am I leading the life I want to live,
Given the vagueness of the pronoun "I,"
The number of things it wants at any moment.

Fictive or not, the soul asks for a few things only,
If not just one. So life would be clearer
If it weren't so silent, inaudible
Even here in the yard an hour past sundown
When the pair of cardinals and crowd of starlings
Have settled down for the night in the poplars.

Have I planted the seed of my talent in fertile soil?
Have I watered and trimmed the sapling?
Do birds nest in my canopy? Do I throw a shade
Others might find inviting? These are some handy metaphors
The soul is free to use if it finds itself
Unwilling to speak directly for reasons beyond me,
Assuming it's eager to be of service.

Now the moon, rising above the branches,
Offers itself to my soul as a double,
Its scarred face an image of the disappointment
I'm ready to say I've caused if the soul
Names the particulars and suggests amendments.

So fine are the threads that the moon
Uses to tug at the ocean that Galileo himself
Couldn't imagine them. He tried to explain the tides
By the earth's momentum as yesterday

I tried to explain my early waking
Three hours before dawn by street noise.

Now I'm ready to posit a tug
Or nudge from the soul. Some insight
Too important to be put off till morning
Might have been mine if I'd opened myself
To the occasion as now I do.

Here's a chance for the soul to fit its truth
To a world of yards, moons, poplars, and starlings,
To resist the fear that to talk my language
Means to be shoehorned into my perspective
Till it thinks as I do, narrowly.

"Be brave, Soul," I want to say to encourage it.
"Your student, however slow, is willing,
The only student you'll ever have."

HALFWAY

Halfway through the novel my friend has written
Where the rash young hero, part white, part Choctaw,
Runs off with the doctor's daughter, I can guess the outcome
Once the girl takes ill after all-night marches
And they rest in an empty cabin for a week or two.
I can guess he'll sense the risk they're running
But will slowly succumb to her innocent hope in safety
Till the posse finds them and a dozen furious citizens
Drag him away despite her protests.
So what if eloping was her idea.
This is rural Mississippi, in 1911, as conceived by my friend,
Who's tried to make his art as faithful to the probable
As true art must be, avoiding the kinds of accidents
That speckle the pages of history, the hairbreadth escapes
That would let the lovers arrive at a rural depot
With seconds to spare before the train to Ohio
Blows its whistle and pulls away.
Art makes the reader care for the characters
And root for a getaway though it won't provide one.
Art offers the joy of watching the lovers
Journey toward insight if not towards freedom
As they talk by their cabin fire, their spirits
Climbing above the doctrines they were taught as children
To a lookout that the posse will never climb to.
From there they can scan their lives spread out like a valley.
Ripeness is all, that's the truth my friend abides by,
Which I admit I'm willing to bend if it helps the lovers
Enjoy more years together. How hard could it be
To provide the sheriff with enough misgivings
To make him hesitate for a crucial moment?
Fine with me if he slowly becomes the hero
So long as the fugitives reach Ohio in safety.
If my friend's forgotten to provide them train fare,

He can add a character to the crowd at the station
Who might credibly offer a loan or gift.
A woman of means, for example, no longer young,
Who's felt firsthand the narrowness of her neighbors
And is touched to observe the lovers inspecting their coins
As if they believed three dollars, counted a hundred times,
Might grow into ten. She's always wanted to get away,
And now by helping them do what she never will
She can put her wishes to use. And if the contrast
Between their luck and her lack of it is painful,
That's the pain we're willing to add to the book
To protect our friends, a substitute sacrifice
The goddess Art rejects as unseemly
Since it costs us nothing.

for Reginald Gibbons

AUDIENCE

When I take the time to read slowly, the words sink in.
If I hadn't rushed my reading of *Anna Karenina*
The first time through, focusing on plot, not nuance,
I might have been able to say why Karenin,
On the night he discovers his wife loves Vronsky,
Gives her a cool lecture on the proprieties
And hides what he feels, how the bridge of his life
Has suddenly fallen away beneath him.
Why does a man who's tumbling into the void
Want to tumble in silence, without a cry?

Now as I drive to visit a friend in the country,
Listening as the story is slowly spoken on tape
By an actress with all the time in the world,
It's clear to me the invisible beings
Karenin imagines watching him from their balcony
Would be embarrassed by any display of feeling.

As to why he's chosen for himself an audience
That judges on the basis of a cool appearance,
Good form, good show, and neglects the soul,
This must be what it means to live in St. Petersburg,
City of courtiers and court ambitions,
And not in Moscow, its country cousin,
Noisy with laughing and crying families.

I'm glad the friend I'm driving to visit
Lives hours away in a country village,
A tolerant woman who won't reproach me
For driving slowly, who'll be glad to learn
I'm taking my own sweet time for reflection.

It's a shame no one enlightened steps forward
To tell Karenin he's a character in a novel
Where no one's commended for preserving his dignity,
Only for shouting and weeping and tearing his hair,
For throwing a book of philosophy out the window.

It looks like I'm one of the fortunate few
With leisure enough to ask myself
If all the invisible beings watching my life
Hail from Moscow. And I'll have time this evening
To ask my friend her honest opinion
And to weigh her answer.
And then it's time to ask if the life she's living
Pleases the beings she imagines watching
And whether they watch from duty or sympathy.

Life would be easier, I'll say, if our audience
Were a single person, like Dante's Beatrice.
Just the thought of her silently looking on
From across a stream was enough to brighten a path
Otherwise forlorn. But how can Dante be sure,
My friend will ask me, that he knows her wishes?
What if they don't all show in her face, or only show
As if veiled by mist, and he sees them darkly?

A LETTER FROM MARY IN THE TYROL

You may believe you're as sorry as you say you are
Not to be hiking with me over mountain meadows,
Sorry your duties at home keep you from travel.
Still, I have to admit I was tempted this afternoon,
As I stood in a guildhall square by a clock tower,
To liken you to the painted soldier
Lurching from his house high in the clock face
To tap the rim of his drum two times.

He looked so full of his mission, so solemn,
As if without his efforts the dome of the sky,
Turning too slow or fast, would begin to wobble,
And crack in the middle, and come crashing down.

All around him the visible face of the landscape
Cried out for attention, the cry I've been hearing
These last few days and answering as best I can
Without the contributions you might have made.

At least I haven't distracted myself from the moment
With thinking of projects I've left half-finished.
At least I know my friends can get on without me,
The gap I've left in their days already closing
While I give my attention to vistas
Far more flamboyant than I imagined.

As I left the square to walk the ramparts,
The soldier was jerking back to his tin house
For another hour of practice.
Three o'clock would be here,
With all its responsibilities, before he knew it.

Is it fair to liken his theory of time to yours?
To me you seem to regard a day as water
Dripping from your cupped fingers,
Each drop a loss you'll have to account for
On the day of judgment you say you don't believe in.

Everyone, to be sure, can use a metaphor.
I don't deny I want to believe this landscape
Has been waiting eons for eyes like mine,
As tender and clear and steady,
And has taken a vow to hold back nothing.

There's nothing wrong with imagining missions
So long as we understand why we choose them,
And approve our motives, and debate alternatives.
Consider our brother in his windowless tin house,
The good it would do him to ask why it seems so fine,
When he could be elsewhere, to wait in the dark,
Shoulders thrown back, for his cue.

NUMBERS

Two hands may not always be better than one,
But four feet and more are likely to prove
More steady than two as we wade a stream
Holding above our heads the ark
Of our covenant with the true and beautiful,
A crowd of outlaw pagans hot on our heels,
The shades of our ancestors cheering us on.

Three friends with poems at Mac's this evening
Are closer than one to the truth if we lift our glasses
To the poet that Mac proposes
We toast before beginning, Li Po.

Three votes that the poem I've brought is finished
Versus one turn of the head too slight
For anyone not on the watch to notice
As Li Po demurs.

Is this America, land of one man, one vote,
I want to ask, or the China of one-man rule,
Of emperors who believe they're gods?

Li Po, now only a thin layer of dust
In Szechwan Province though somehow
Still standing inches behind his words.

Five of my lines, he suggests with a nod,
Out of the score I've written,
Are fine as they are if I provide them

The context that they deserve and speak them
Without misgivings and with greater gusto.

Five lead out from the kitchen
Past a dozen detours to a single bridge
That must be crossed in order to reach a homeland
Eager for my arrival.

This is the message I get from a prophet whose signs
Are a threadbare coat and an empty cupboard,
Proof he's never written for anyone but himself
And the dead teachers easy to count
On the stiff fingers of one hand.

In memory of Mac Hammond

THE FALLEN

Now that a year's gone by since your enemy
From childhood on, implacable diabetes,
Finally defeated you, it's time for you to appear
In dream, your sight restored, your indignant beard
Peaceably trimmed, your prophet's brow,
Creased before by the world's injustices,
Smooth as you take a chair at my bedside.

You'll have come to tell me the relief I felt
When your heart gave out after a day at the hospital
Was only natural, natural for a friend
Who was glad you'd given the slip at last
To a body that was never loyal,
To a servant plotting still more betrayals.

With a doctor's graceful bedside manner, you'll say
That if I begrudged you an extra portion of sympathy
I have nothing to be ashamed of.
Your loneliness must have felt to me like a pit
Too vast to be filled, while duties more doable
Called for attention, and I wanted to make a difference,
To see in people around me proof of my power.

There's a time for remorse, your ghost will explain,
And a time to believe the future offers occasions
More ample than those yet offered
For making improvements and moving on.

I'm listening to the speech I'm having you make
About the forgiveness filling your heart
Even if I was common enough to wish
Simply to spend my leisure in cheerier company,
With friends less retrospective, distant, and death-bound.

You're linking my lapse to the lapse that Milton, your hero,
Attributed to the pair who brought Eden down.

The will, I'm waiting for you to say, is composed
Of many voices, and of these only one
Can be labeled fallen, one selfish voice
Clamoring for the floor in the chamber of voices
When the soul convenes far enough from the street
To hear itself debating.

Just one sleek speaker who argues the point
That the suffering overseas is a quagmire
Best avoided, however pure our intentions.
A voice that more often than not
Fails to persuade the others, and when it succeeds
Leaves them all feeling small and stingy.

In memory of Burton Weber

EURYDICE

If the dead could speak, I'd entreat you
Not to blame yourself for losing me near the exit.
I was gone before you turned to glimpse me.
Your hope I would follow you into the light—
That was only a poet's faith in the power of music.
I followed as far as the law of Hell allowed me
And then turned back to my dark home.
For us to live together, you'd have to descend
Again to the place that chills the heart of the living.
I wouldn't want you to lie awake beside me
Straining to look on the bright side,
Spinning out plan after plan full of adventure.
I wouldn't want you to wait with patience
For my reply, to assume my lengthening silence
A thoughtful prologue. The hours would grow into years
While you dreamed up a song about our ascent
Meant for the ears of friends on our arrival.
I wouldn't want to hear it dwindle and fade
As the truth gradually came into focus
And you slowly deferred to a greater power.
Who would you be then? No one I know,
Not the man who thought his music enlarged creation.
If I could speak, child of the sun,
I'd assure you I'm still your wife.
That's why I want you to stay as long as you can
Just as you are, the mistaken
Hopeful man I married.

THE LACE MAKER

Holding the bobbins taut as she moves the pins,
She leans in close, inches away from the fabric
Fretted and framed on the wooden work board.

A young woman in a yellow dress
Whose lighter hair, bound tight to her head
But flowing about one shoulder,

Suggests the self-forgetful beauty of service,
Service to a discipline. Just so the painting
Forgets the background to focus on her.

Here she is, so close to the surface
The painter could touch her if he stretched his hand.
Close work in sympathy with close work.

The sewing cushion holding the colored threads
Suggests a painter's palette. So Vermeer
Offers a silent tribute to another artist

Who's increasing the number of beautiful
Useless things available in a world
That would be darker and smaller without them.

This is no time to ask if the woman
Wishes she were rich enough to buy the likeness,
If Vermeer can afford the lace she's making;

No time to consider them bandying compliments.
They work in silence, and you may look on
Only if you quiet your thoughts enough

To hear the click of her needles as you lean in close
(But not so close that you cast a shadow)
And the light touch of his brush on canvas.

AFTER EDEN

When my neighbor in Eden needed to muse
Alone for a week in a hut by the ocean,
She could rely, without having to ask, on me
To water her garden, me and my natural kindness.

But here before she can wave good-bye
She needs to hear me say, "I promise,"
I promise to resist my natural inclination
To put things off, or away, or lose them.

In Eden good feelings were good enough.
Here they require support from a contract
I have to honor if I want to consider myself
Someone whose word may be relied on.

To promise, to say a particular deed
Isn't merely likely, given my generous spirit,
But inscribed in the history of my life to come,
Which may be amended by fate but not by me.

And if fate steps in to pull me away from town,
My promise means I'll appoint a substitute
Who'll promise to embrace the task just as it is,
Who won't presume to offer amendments.

No arguing that my neighbor's overindulged her garden,
That her coddled sprigs are due for a little tough love,
The discipline of neglect, till they realize
How ungrateful they've been for their many blessings.

In Eden she'd say with a good-bye hug,
"Water them whenever you think they need it."

Here she tears from her lined notebook, legal size,
A sheet of numbered instructions. Item one:

Don't lose this list. Tape it to your mirror
However foolish it makes you feel
To see it beside your face in the morning,
A blurry human face that needs defining.

PROGRESS

This is the shadowy god who advises patience,
Who asks you to be content, for the moment,
With a ramshackle motel in the boondocks,
To believe it's one of the way stations on the road
To a land your successors will consider promised.

For them you should try to accept the sag in your mattress,
The smell of mildew, the frost on the floor,
The empty wood box. If you're cold,
You can always go out in the yard
And chop your own. The exercise
Will be good for you, the fresh air.

Even a scruffy patch by a railroad crossing
Can serve, since travel is mainly a metaphor,
As a site not yet developed in the next Jerusalem.
Here's your chance to get in on the ground floor
Of a temple soon to be under construction.
Or even beneath the floor as you dig the foundation,
Standing knee-deep in muck on the very spot
Where, overhead, your descendants will dance
To music more festive than any you now imagine.

How small of you to dicker with the foreman
When to work for nothing would be a privilege.
As for diversions that you won't have time for—
Summer picnics, fall fishing at sunrise
These are mere shadows of pleasures to come
That others will savor because of you
As others have lived in debt to Aeneas or Moses.

Jacob, who toiled seven years for the woman he loved,
Then seven more, is nothing compared to you,

You who toil so somebody not yet born
Can marry a woman you've never laid eyes on.

Do it, and the god of progress will love you
As his own child. Don't vex him by wondering
If the prince will impress the princess as much
As she would you, if he'll like the palace
You're building for him or prefer instead
To live in a shack with a Jezebel who informs him
Tomorrow's for losers, better grab today.

PROGRESSIVE HEALTH

We here at Progressive Health would like to thank you
For being one of the generous few who've promised
To bequeath your vital organs to whoever needs them.

Now we'd like to give you the opportunity
To step out far in front of the other donors
By acting a little sooner than you expected,

Tomorrow, to be precise, the day you're scheduled
To come in for your yearly physical. Six patients
Are waiting this very minute in intensive care

Who will likely die before another liver
And spleen and pairs of lungs and kidneys
Match theirs as closely as yours do. Twenty years,

Maybe more, are left you, granted, but the gain
Of these patients might total more than a century.
To you, of course, one year of your life means more

Than six of theirs, but to no one else,
No one as concerned with the general welfare
As you've claimed to be. As for your poems—

The few you may have it in you to finish—
Even if we don't judge them by those you've written,
Even if we assume you finally stage a breakthrough,

It's doubtful they'll raise one Lazarus from a grave
Metaphoric or literal. But your body is guaranteed
To work six wonders. As for the gaps you'll leave

As an aging bachelor in the life of friends,
They'll close far sooner than the open wounds
Soon to be left in the hearts of husbands and wives,

Parents and children, by the death of the six
Who now are failing. Just imagine how grateful
They'll all be when they hear of your grand gesture.

Summer and winter they'll visit your grave, in shifts,
For as long as they live, and stoop to tend it,
And leave it adorned with flowers or holly wreaths,

While your friends, who are just as forgetful
As you are, just as liable to be distracted,
Will do no more than a makeshift job of upkeep.

If the people you'll see tomorrow pacing the halls
Of our crowded facility don't move you enough,
They'll make you at least uneasy. No happy future

Is likely in store for a man like you whose conscience
Will ask him to certify every hour from now on
Six times as full as it was before, your work

Six times as strenuous, your walks in the woods
Six times as restorative as anyone else's.
Why be a drudge, staggering to the end of your life

Under this crushing burden when, with a single word,
You could be a god, one of the few gods
Who, when called on, really listens?

JUST DESERTS

Don't we still worship the goddess Justice,
Still believe the race goes to the swift,
The literal race if not the metaphoric,
Run on the local track when the wind is gentle,
The cinders firm and dry and level,
And a senior coach like Mr. Ruggieri
Stands at the finish line, stopwatch in hand,
Unbiased and incorruptible?

A gray-haired, soft-voiced man in a warm-up jacket
With a gift for spotting talent and bringing it forward,
Who wonders, as his last semester approaches,
If his gift might have been exercised in a field
Far more ample if he'd been smarter or luckier.
It seems a shame we can't offer him something
More heartening than a farewell banquet
With its testimonies of lasting appreciation.

It would be more like justice if we could assure him
The story he's nearly done with, set mainly in Buffalo,
Was meant as a restful interlude after his busy life
As prince of Parma and before the Asian adventures
Destined for his soul. A balm to say he's forgotten
The reception hall of Parian marble
Where every morning he lent his ear to petitioners,
The lowliest first, as his love for justice demanded.

After that, why not this stint as coach in a high school
While the parents to be next assigned him
Are born and raised in a village near Srinagar
Where later they'll meet and marry to the sound of chimes
Swaying in the breeze that cools the temple.
Twelve years from that day their son will be registered

In the temple school to study the holy arts
Of meditation and praise, of walking
From valley to mountain shrine
In the company of his staff and begging bowl.

Wouldn't these words to Mr. Ruggieri
After the banquet, as we drive him home,
Be just what's wanted to lift his spirits?
Then when he sat alone in his bedroom,
He'd be prepared if the shoes set by the bed
Looked lost in a dream of mountain trails
He'd never show them. "Just you wait,"
He could tell them; "just you be patient.
Your time is coming."

MORE ART

Why drive home to your empty house and your plans,
Still vague, for grasping life by the forelock
When across the street from the bank where your job
In home loans may soon prove expendable
The action's already begun on the big screen
Of the Granger Theater. Come watch
As a pale-faced stewardess runs down the aisle
To the row where a man sits with a notebook
Long past midnight, when everyone else is sleeping.
He's taken this flight from Spokane to Cleveland
More than a hundred times without incident;
But now as he tinkers with his five-part program
For safe investments and early retirement,
He feels a hand on his shoulder, and looking up
Faces the pale stewardess, who motions him forward,
Up to the cockpit. The pilot has had a stroke
And the drunk copilot can't be wakened.
So the man, who looks from your vantage point
High in the balcony like your brother Herman,
Straps himself in to confront, five miles above Ohio,
A yard-high panel of flashing lights
While a crackly voice comes over the radio.
It's the flight controller, Miss Wu,
Who promises to lead him step by step
To a happy landing, though her wobbling pitch
Suggests she's never before talked anyone down.
Hard for you to sit still and watch in silence
Given your joy that a man who drove to the airport
Two hours early, fearful of heavy traffic,
Is having a real adventure thrust upon him.
Now above the static he hears the sound of rustling
As Miss Wu unfolds a drawing of the instrument screen
The better to tell him how to control his wobbling.

And then the scene shifts to her desk, the photograph
Of her young father, newly arrived from China,
Ready to scrimp and save so his baby girl
Can go to school as long as she wants to.
And then the camera lifts to the girl grown up,
Her face intent as she gives directions,
Her hair tied in a ponytail. From your seat it's clear
She looks less like the cherished daughter of Mr. Lee,
The owner of Northtown Hardware, and more like a twin
Of the girl who irons your shirts in the Granger laundry
A block from the theater. An orphan, you heard once,
When you asked the owner, for you've been curious
And now you know why. Someone should bring her here
To watch as her sister urges your brother the pilot
Not to lose hope as the houses below, small a moment ago,
Loom suddenly large. Look around for a makeshift runway.
Look for the switch that lowers the landing gear.
This is the way to learn, right on the job,
From a teacher with a soft, musical voice
That makes you glad you're not at home by the phonograph
Trying to teach yourself to dance with a broom,
Your self-help chart of the steps taped to the floor.

BASHŌ

When my tastes seem too haphazard and disjointed
To compose a character, it's a comfort
To think of them as inherited from my ancestors,
Each expressing through me ancient inflections.

My need before supper to stroll to the reservoir
May indicate on my father's side nomadic origins,
The blood of a captive from Scythia who was sold
To a family in Lombardy in need of a plowman.

His marriage to a slave girl from Carthage
Explains why sea air smells so familiar,
Why I like the look of whitewashed houses on hillsides
And painted tile from Tunisia or Morocco.

To be a vehicle for the dead to speak through,
Surely that's an improvement over being a showman
Who shifts his costume to please a moody audience.
It's a comfort as long as I've many dead to choose from,

Free to trace my talent for telling stories
At a moment's notice in the style of Odysseus
All the way back on my mother's side
To a black-bearded Smyrna merchant.

His skill makes me a star at the tourist bureau
When I'm asked for ideas to make Lake Erie
More glamorous than it is in the current brochures,
The photographs more arresting, the copy spicier.

Good thing for the tourists I've also inherited
Truth-telling genes from the Hebrew prophets

That keep me from claiming our seagulls special,
As musical as the nightingale and as retiring.

So many dispositions, but no reason to worry
About caulking and splicing them into unity.
Each ancient voice asks to be kept distinct,
A separate species of tree in a crowded forest,

Cedar and pine, oak, ash, and cherry.
It isn't an accident, as I sit in the yard reading poems
Under the hemlock, that I'm drawn to Bashō.
It's clear that his blood flows in my veins,

Clear he's my father or else my twin
Misplaced at birth in a shorthanded village hospital.
How else explain that a poem of his
Is nearer to me than the proverbs of seven uncles?

Witness the first haiku in the new translation
I bought this morning at Niagara Books:
"Even in Kyoto, hearing the cuckoo's cry,
I long for Kyoto."

IMPROBABLE STORY

Far from here, in the probable world,
The stable reign of the dinosaurs
Hasn't been brought to a sudden, unlooked-for end
By a billion-to-one crash with an asteroid
Ten miles across at impact, or a comet.

No dust cloud there darkens the sky
Till it snuffs out half the kingdom of vegetation,
As it might in a B movie from Hollywood,
And half the animal families,
The heavy feeders and breathers among them.

The dinosaurs rule the roost over there,
And the mammals, forced to keep hidden,
Only survive as pygmies. No time for the branching
That leads to us. None of our lean-tos or igloos,
Churches or silos, dot the landscape,

No schools or prisons. Not a single porch
Where you can sit as you're sitting here
Writing to Martha that your fog has lifted,
That despite the odds against transformation
You've left the age of ambivalence far behind you.

Over there, in the probable world, your "yes"
Means what it always has, "Who knows?"
Your "maybe" means that your doubts are overwhelming.
Martha doesn't believe one sentence as she reads
In the shade of a willow that could never survive

The winter's killer ice storms. No purple martins return
In the probable world to the little house you made them,
Ready to eat in a week their weight in mosquitoes

While Martha completes a letter that over there
She'll never be foolish enough to begin.

BISHOP BERKELEY

Maybe the material world would have seemed to him
Real enough, his doubts mostly illusion,
If his boyhood had been less bookish.
Maybe if he'd grown up on a farm,
A glass of milk left on his desk by a servant
To help him ease into sleep would have seemed like more
Than a prop in a play, and the wall of books behind it
Would have looked more solid than a painted backdrop.
The glass might have recalled his milking days,
The boy in the barn with Madge, the Guernsey.
Few arguments then could have convinced him
That he merely dreamed the warmth of her fur,
The ripe barn smell, the weight of the pail
As he carried it, waving the flies away, to the kitchen.
Then the Bishop might have turned his philosophy
To questions a farmer might ask on Sunday evening
Like the deepest difference between the perspective of cows
And that of the man who keeps the herd.
Is it their failure to guess the fate that awaits them
While we, intent on the truth, guess ours,
Or do they know something unknown to us
That keeps them quiet and uncomplaining,
Free of the wish for triumph or travel? Even today
A farmer might read that chapter with profit
Before he turns to wonder why his wife's awakened
Each morning for three weeks running with a dream of Prague,
The city she left with her family when she was five.
Why have those buried images shaken loose
From the bottom of the pond just now, after thirty years,
And floated up till the woman won't rest
Till she compares the city she still recalls
To the one that's bound to be disappointing?
Soon near the outskirts of Prague, in a budget motel,

The farmer will lie beside her listening to the road noise.
It's too far for him to glimpse the roof of his barn,
Which the Bishop doesn't think solid anyway,
But he can almost hear, when the traffic slows,
The sound of the cows crossing the gravel path,
And then their softer steps on the grass of the pasture,
And then their stillness as they bend to browse.

SUNRISE

The Aztecs may not, after all, have been brutal
Though they believed the sun wouldn't rise
Unless the shrines of the sun god reeked with the odor
Of human blood. Maybe their notion of debt
Was stricter than ours. What could they pay the sun
For the priceless gift of corn but men and women
With their lives before them, young and happy?

As for a god who didn't expect repayment,
Who was happy to give as long as our species
Showed it was grateful, more a parent than lender—
That notion was no more rational than the other
And far less likely to explain disaster,
Though in the long run it proved as practical
As other great inventions, the lever, the wheel.

Just the token first fruits of the field,
Just the firstlings among the calves and lambs
Sacrificed in the Temple to the sound of chanting.
And when the Romans pulled the Temple down,
The scattered worshipers decided upon a god
Who was willing to come with them into exile,
To forgo his rich diet of cattle
And make do with a bowl of peas or lentils
Left in the night at the door of a widow's cottage.

For a god so loyal, his people were willing
To overlook his inability to protect them,
Taking the blame on themselves instead.
And didn't their refusal to cast a shadow

On his reputation for justice win them an extra
Ounce of forgiveness when they tried his patience?

They tried his patience on days when the law
Felt to them like a burden, not like blessing,
But by most evenings they'd worked their way,
Grumbling, back to acceptance. And at night,
Worn out from the effort, they slept hard,
And hours later were sleeping still
When the sun god they didn't worship
Rose in the dark on his own to feed his horses,
Just as his sunny nature prompted,
And hitch his golden chariot.

ETERNAL POETRY

How to grow old with grace and firmness
Is the kind of eternal problem that poetry
Is best reserved for, unaging poetry
That isn't afraid of saying what time will do
To our taste and talents, our angles of observation.
As for a local problem mentioned in passing
In this morning's news, like the cut in food stamps,
It's handled more effectively in an essay
With graphs and numbers. A poem's no proper place
To dwell on the prison reforms my friend proposes
Based on his twenty-year stint inside the walls.
In an essay there's room to go into details
So the State of New York can solve the problem
Once and for all and turn to issues more lasting.
Facing old age, the theme I'm developing here,
Will still be an issue when the failure of prisons
Interests only historians of our backward era.
A poem's the thing for grappling with the question
Whether it's best to disdain old age as a pest
Or respect it as a mighty army or welcome it
As a guest with a ton of baggage. Three options
That health-care professionals might deem too harsh
To appear in their journals. I wish they would help
My friend publish his essay on prison reform,
His practical plan to inspire the inmates
By cutting their minimum sentences if they master a trade
So they won't return, as is likely now, in a year or two.
The odds are long against getting the ear of the governor
But not impossible if he's only a year from retirement
And old age prompts him to earn a paragraph
In the history of reform. The bill might squeak through
If the Assembly decides it hasn't the wherewithal
To keep the old prisons in decent repair

Let alone build new ones. No money now
To pay the prison inspector what he deserves
As he makes his rounds in his battered pickup.
An old man shaking his head in disgust
At the roof leaks, peeling plaster, and rusty plumbing
That might have been avoided with a little foresight
And therefore don't deserve a place in a poem.
And to think he's been at it for thirty years
Despite his vow, after a month on the job,
To be out of it at the latest by Christmas.
Nobody's eager to wear his shoes
Unless we count the people inside the walls
Whose envy of those growing old outside
Is a constant always to be relied on,
And so can enter a poem at any time.

IN THE SHORT TERM

There's no denying that the only joy
Likely to last lies in our power completely,
As the Stoics say, not in the power of others.

The joy, for example, of placing one's life in harmony
With laws that reason deduces to be eternal,
Of doing our work as it should be done—
No cutting corners to speed delivery,
No rushing to finish the job before closing time.
No closing time, in fact, so long as the work is pleasing.

The joy of winning glory among one's fellows,
However sweet, lasts only until the fellows
Sail off for better jobs across the ocean.
Lucky for them if they learn to become
The citizens of the world that the Stoics say
We should all become, not Romans any longer,
Not Egyptians, Medes, or Athenians.

There's no denying applause-loving Alcibiades
Is like a man who builds a magnificent tower
On sand, that the tower in falling
Crushes his neighbors' roofs as well as his own.
Shame on him for wrecking the peace talks with Sparta
So he could contrive the war he longed to shine in
And be cheered the loudest when he strolled the agora.

An hour after his fleet set sail for Sicily, his enemies,
In envy of all the glory soon to be his, were working
To turn the minds of the crowd against him.
Too bad he didn't listen to Socrates
On the rational soul and the nourishment it requires,

Different from praise, to become immortal,
The praise that Homer was wrong to bestow on war.

There's no denying insight to Epictetus
When he argues the story of Troy is about illusion,
That Paris was crazy to endanger his town for the sheen
Of a woman's body, Helen crazy to love a playboy,
Menelaus to think that a wife as light as his
Worth regaining. As for Achilles, whatever possessed him
To squabble with Agamemnon over a war prize?

All dust now, Troy as much as the flesh of Helen
Though Homer never assumes they're immortal,
Just that you won't be likely to forget them quickly
Once their story is told in the leisurely way
It should be told, over many evenings.

Time enough to make clear that fault-ridden Paris
Is loved by a goddess, that Helen's a gift
Only a goddess could have provided.
And who is he to deny a goddess
Even if her gift only lasts a day?

Guardian Angel

Not the angel that helps you resist temptation
(Conscience and heart are enough for that,
And, besides, when have you been tempted lately?),
But the one with advice about tactics
For possessing your share of the true and beautiful.
The one who tells you the plaid of your jacket
Will prove too loud for the soft-spoken sensitive woman
You're destined to meet tonight in line at the theater
When everything depends on a first impression.

With the angel's help you can open a conversation
On a fruitful subject like happiness and explain
People are wrong to seek it directly,
How it comes on the back of other things
Like losing oneself in a casual conversation
That tests our powers of empathy, not cleverness.

A practical angel, ignorant in philosophy
But peerless in group dynamics, who can show you
Why it's unwise to urge your hesitant friend
To leave her apartment for yours too quickly,
How a sudden fear of confinement may choke off feelings
That otherwise would be sure to bloom.

And if eagerness wins out over prudence, the angel,
Instead of saying, "I told you so," will help you
Turn from errors that can't be altered
And sally out in quest of a local problem
Where your many talents can make a difference.

Why not get involved with the block-club committee
Dedicated to stopping the corner drugstore
From tripling in size and knocking down in the process

Houses that keep the scale of the neighborhood human?
Soon you may find yourself toasting the cause
By candlelight with your eager co-chair,
A woman fearless in the face of officialdom.

It's true if she had an angel to help her
She wouldn't be wearing the dress she's wearing,
A duplicate of the one your mother wore
Thirty summers ago at Cape May when your father
Embarked full-time on his career of drinking.
But doesn't this ignorance, which her angel
Should have dispelled, make her appealing
To someone like you, who's quick to discern a soul mate?

As you sit across the table you can feel your heart
Swell with so much sympathy that your jacket
Feels tight in the chest, your loud plaid jacket.
"Why not remove it," the angel you need would ask,
"And drape it out of sight on the back of your chair?"

MAY JEN

This is the evening I was hoping for,
The one when my bad times are transposed to stories
Offered as a small return for the story you've just told me
Here at this window table in the May Jen restaurant
On rain-washed Elmwood. How once,
When drink had driven your dad from the family,
Meeting you on the street, he gave you his promise,
In a voice cold sober, to send you the dress
You needed for confirmation, and how you felt
When it never arrived. A sad story
That makes me happy I've carried for years
Memories that till this evening I've never valued.

This is the rainy April evening toward which our lives,
Despite the odds, have been moving for decades
Along different paths, without our knowing,
So we might notice through this rain-streaked window
How the glinting streetlamps and street reflections,
Stoplights and traffic, set off by contrast
Our easy calm, our stillness.

This is the conversation that can have no midpoint,
However clear its beginning, if it has no end.
And why would we turn to ask for the bill,
Why don our raincoats and walk to the car
And join the pitiful traffic that has to make do
With the dream of a life behind it or a life ahead?
The past we need is only a kind of currency
Stamped in red with the date of this day.
And the fabulous future is beginning to understand
If it wants to meet us it will have to swallow its pride
And come to our table, not wait for us to come looking,
For we have no plans to go anywhere.

ETERNAL LIFE

An immortal soul, that's something for me to wish for,
To be off on a long trek after my body's buried
And my friends have driven away from the graveyard.

Where am I headed? Not downward, if I'm permitted
To judge by the rules of fairness as I conceive them,
For nothing I've done seems ripe for eternal punishment.

Not upward, for nothing seems worthy of eternal bliss.
Odds are I'll stay where I am, forever earthbound,
And face the problem of filling the endless return

Of earthly summers and autumns, winters and springs.
It won't be easy for a being retired from action,
A shadow too weak even to hold open a door

When a friend among the living, bearing a tea tray,
Comes to join her guests on the verandah.
The conversation should hold my interest all evening

Even if I can't participate, my voice too small.
But later, when strangers fill the familiar rooms,
I'll seem to be listening to a script that's conventional,

To acting forced and wooden, and slip outside.
What then? Do I keep my distance from other ghosts
Or join them in sharing stories about the old days

In cricket whispers? Either way, I'll wonder about the joy
I imagined coming my way with death behind me,
Not looming ahead, and leisure, so scarce before,

Suddenly limitless. Not much solace is likely
When I compare the vague ghosts of my friends
With the living originals, whose particular lusters

Can't be divorced from their lifelong gloom on birthdays,
Their protests against their mirrors, their witty admissions
In listing the enemies that creased their foreheads

And slowed their pace to a hobble, and made them forgetful,
Though they remembered their promises well enough
And tried to keep many till death released them.

But how can ghosts swear loyalty to the end
If there is no end for them, only a boundless ocean;
Or does a truth I haven't a map to now

Wait in my ghostly existence to be discovered? If not,
It won't surprise me if I find myself on my knees
Cupping my hands with others at the river's edge

To sip forgetfulness. No surprise if I'm ferried back,
Oblivious, to be born again in the flesh
Among strangers it will take me years to recognize.

The God Who Loves You

It must be troubling for the god who loves you
To ponder how much happier you'd be today
Had you been able to glimpse your many futures.
It must be painful for him to watch you on Friday evenings
Driving home from the office, content with your week—
Three fine houses sold to deserving families—
Knowing as he does exactly what would have happened
Had you gone to your second choice for college,
Knowing the roommate you'd have been allotted
Whose ardent opinions on painting and music
Would have kindled in you a lifelong passion.
A life thirty points above the life you're living
On any scale of satisfaction. And every point
A thorn in the side of the god who loves you.
You don't want that, a large-souled man like you
Who tries to withhold from your wife the day's disappointments
So she can save her empathy for the children.
And would you want this god to compare your wife
With the woman you were destined to meet on the other campus?
It hurts you to think of him ranking the conversation
You'd have enjoyed over there higher in insight
Than the conversation you're used to.
And think how this loving god would feel
Knowing that the man next in line for your wife
Would have pleased her more than you ever will
Even on your best days, when you really try.
Can you sleep at night believing a god like that
Is pacing his cloudy bedroom, harassed by alternatives
You're spared by ignorance? The difference between what is
And what could have been will remain alive for him
Even after you cease existing, after you catch a chill
Running out in the snow for the morning paper,
Losing eleven years that the god who loves you

Will feel compelled to imagine scene by scene
Unless you come to the rescue by imagining him
No wiser than you are, no god at all, only a friend
No closer than the actual friend you made at college,
The one you haven't written in months. Sit down tonight
And write him about the life you can talk about
With a claim to authority, the life you've witnessed,
Which for all you know is the life you've chosen.

photo credit: Rayna Knobler

ABOUT THE AUTHOR

Carl Dennis is the author of seven other books of poetry, including, most recently, *Ranking the Wishes*. A recipient of fellowships from the Guggenheim Foundation and the National Endowment for the Arts, in 2000 he was awarded the Ruth Lilly Prize from *Poetry Magazine* and the Modern Poetry Association for his contribution to American poetry. He teaches in the English Department at the State University of New York at Buffalo, and is a sometime member of the faculty of the MFA program in creative writing at Warren Wilson College.

Ted Berrigan	*Selected Poems*
Ted Berrigan	*The Sonnets*
Philip Booth	*Lifelines*
Philip Booth	*Pairs*
Jim Carroll	*Fear of Dreaming*
Jim Carroll	*Void of Course*
Nicholas Christopher	*5° & Other Poems*
Carl Dennis	*Practical Gods*
Carl Dennis	*Ranking the Wishes*
Diane di Prima	*Loba*
Stuart Dischell	*Evenings and Avenues*
Stephen Dobyns	*Common Carnage*
Stephen Dobyns	*Pallbearers Envying the One Who Rides*
Paul Durcan	*A Snail in My Prime*
Amy Gerstler	*Crown of Weeds*
Amy Gerstler	*Medicine*
Amy Gerstler	*Nerve Storm*
Debora Greger	*Desert Fathers, Uranium Daughters*
Debora Greger	*God*
Robert Hunter	*Glass Lunch*
Robert Hunter	*Sentinel*
Barbara Jordan	*Trace Elements*
Jack Kerouac	*Book of Blues*
Ann Lauterbach	*And For Example*
Ann Lauterbach	*If In Time: Selected Poems 1975–2000*
Ann Lauterbach	*On a Stair*
Phillis Levin	*Mercury*
William Logan	*Night Battle*
William Logan	*Vain Empires*
Derek Mahon	*Selected Poems*
Michael McClure	*Huge Dreams: San Francisco and Beat Poems*
Michael McClure	*Three Poems*
Carol Muske	*An Octave Above Thunder*
Alice Notley	*The Descent of Alette*
Alice Notley	*Disobedience*
Alice Notley	*Mysteries of Small Houses*
Lawrence Raab	*The Probable World*
Anne Waldman	*Kill or Cure*
Anne Waldman	*Marriage: A Sentence*
Rachel Wetzsteon	*Home and Away*
Philip Whalen	*Overtime: Selected Poems*
Robert Wrigley	*In the Bank of Beautiful Sins*
Robert Wrigley	*Reign of Snakes*